THE ABC's OF GLOBAL LEADERSHIP

RUSS CLINE & RON CLINE

EDITED BY TRB CREATION

ISBN: 978-1-935256-16-8

Published by L'Edge Press
A ministry of Upside Down Ministries, Inc.
P.O. Box 2567
Boone, NC 28607

Dedication

This book is dedicated to the Leaders, Partners and Coaches that have been a part of the Leader Mundial Global Leadership Summit. It's been a thrill to journey together as a community these past 5 years. This book is a product of our time together. We've learned and processed through the ABC's, and now we're all a part of taking this training to leaders around the world. Thank you for multiplying what God is doing in your lives into the lives of others.

—Russ & Ron

Introduction

I (Russ) remember years ago sitting with a guy who I considered a powerful leader. He was being used by God in incredible ways and he was impacting thousands of lives. As we shared some time together, he told me that he was ready to quit. I was surprised as this was not what I was expecting. I knew of the pressure he was under, but I didn't know it had gotten to that point. As we talked, he shared that his vision was solid and he was passionate about the goal of impacting lives; however, as the ministry grew, he was being taken further and further away from the front lines. He was leading and developing a board, raising money, managing staff, developing resources, filing legal documents, and managing conflict. He shared that he had been trained and equipped to disciple young people, not to run an organization, and the larger the organization grew, the more pressure he was feeling.

This story is not unique. All of us have experienced this kind of thing as we wrestle with the call God has placed on our lives, and the reality of bringing a vision to reality. As we connected with this leader, we realized that if we could put some people around him, if we could provide some resources for him, and if we could provide some training for him, he would make it. He did make it. He made some changes, he realized that he wasn't alone, and he continues to make adjustments in balancing a growing organization and using his gifts and abilities to disciple young people.

We have found hundreds of leaders just like this around the world, and while each story is different, they are each desperate for training that will help them manage the load. They are desperate for people who understand a little of what they're going through. They are desperate to know that they aren't alone and that there are tools, resources, and training available.

"The ABC's of Global Leadership" was developed for these kinds of Global Leaders.

A "Global Leader" is a leader who is strategically placed around the world for a specific purpose. These leaders have a call from God. These leaders have passion to impact the people they are in position to impact. These leaders think in terms of the "Kingdom of God" instead of building their own kingdom.

As we have had the opportunity to travel, to encourage these leaders, and to come alongside them, we began to think of the training that many of them needed, and out of this was born the "ABC's of Global Leadership."

These 26 words are not all encompassing. They are simply words that jumped out at us as words that we wanted to spend some time unpacking. We juggled the words, we replaced words, we struggled to choose some of them, but these are the words that we ended up with and as we've taught them to groups of leaders, God has used these studies to remind us of some things that we have forgotten.

Global Leaders are often far too busy to take some time to stop, reflect and evaluate. We are encouraging leaders everywhere to do some self-evaluation and to always be learning more about leadership and about the kind of leader God has created and positioned you to be.

As you work through the alphabet, we challenge you to take the time to not only study God's Word on each letter, but also to evaluate how you're doing as a leader with each specific word.

We have learned so much about our own leadership styles in working through these words; we trust that you will as well.

Enjoy the journey!
Russ Cline & Ron Cline
Leadon Esource

Table of Contents

A Leader Has To Be
AWARE

In this day, a leader needs to be aware:
- Of his purpose and skills
- Of his weaknesses
- Of the needs around him
- Of the strengths of his team
- Of God's direction
- Of the requirements of leadership
- Of the resources available
- Of the partnerships available
- Of God's involvement
- Of the expectations of his partners
- Of the power of prayer
- Of the meaning of success

We are past the day of the lone worker trying to change the world. There are too many others and too many resources for that to be necessary or even possible.

To make it work, the leader has to be aware of all these things, plus others. Starting with an awareness of himself, his purpose, his motivation and his skills…and those around him.

Awareness involves many things, but most of all it involves genuine interest and concern as well as intentional attention. You have to care. You have to be there.

It's nice that we start the 26 Traits of Global Leadership with this quality because it will cause all the others to come to life.

A Lesson From The Word

Nehemiah 1:1-4 (NIV) "The words of Nehemiah son of Hacaliah: In the month of Kislev in the twentieth year, while I was in the citadel of Susa, Hanani, one of my brothers, came from Judah with some other men, and I questioned them about the Jewish remnant that survived the exile, and also about Jerusalem. They said to me, 'Those who survived the exile and are back in the province are in great trouble and disgrace. The wall of Jerusalem is broken down, and its gates have been burned with fire.' When I heard these things, I sat down and wept. For some days I mourned and fasted and prayed before the God of heaven."

Nehemiah asked the heavy question, "How are you?" and he listened to the answer. He asked what was happening in Jerusalem, where some Jews had stayed during the exile. He not only asked but he wanted to know, so he listened carefully to the answer.

His response was from his heart. He mourned and he prayed.

That gave time for God to speak to him. He listened. He acted!

As a result he became an agent for God and went to Jerusalem and helped the people there catch the vision to rebuild the city walls.

That unified the people, renewed their faith, and pushed back the enemies. It also rebuilt the walls of the city of God.

All because he made sure he was aware before he moved.

How Awareness Will Affect The Global Leader

Throughout history, people have asked of God, "Are you there? Are you aware? Do you care?" When He answers "Yes" to those questions, and proves it with His presence, we can then live in peace.

The same is asked of leaders by their followers, by their co-workers, and by their partners:
- "Are you aware of all that is involved?"
- "Are you aware of all the needs so that you are responding to the right ones?"
- "Do you care about me and what concerns me?"
- "Are you aware of our commitments and abilities?"

Everyone has a vision for something. Do you know what your fellow workers, what your donors, what your partners really care about? Are you aware of their hopes and dreams?

If you don't take the time to know what people want or what they need, then how can you decide direction, goals, and how to respond to the needs?

You may end up doing what you want for the wrong reason and miss what God wants. What a waste of good work that would be!

God has an amazing way of speaking to us through the advice and comments of others. He may only direct you as you listen to what those around you are saying.

Action Steps

1. Learn to ask instead of tell!

The art of discovering new things is directly linked to the art of asking questions. Spend your next social activity asking about the lives and ideas from the other people there. Learn to ask questions and let their answers direct your next question.

2. Practice listening instead of talking!

Try repeating back to the other person what you think you heard them say. Be aware that you may not have understood or you may not have heard every aspect of what was said. There are so many distractions, it is sometimes very hard to focus on what the other person is saying. Sometimes we even start thinking of our response before they are through speaking.

3. Spend time thinking about what you heard and its impact on others.

Take time to think before you respond. Nehemiah spent days praying about and mourning what he had heard. That gave him time to receive God's direction. He didn't come up with his own ideas and plans, he heard from God and became His agent! You don't have to have an immediate response to a given situation…you need to be aware of God's direction.

A Leader Has To Be BOLD

Have you ever been around a leader who could not make a decision? Or a leader who was afraid to move ahead?

Would you follow a leader who didn't know where he was going? Or why he was doing it? Or how he was going to do it? Would you want a leader filled with fear or discouragement?

There is a very fine line between a leader who is bold and confident and a leader who is proud and arrogant, but there is a difference and that difference is the difference between success and failure.

Godly boldness and courage to follow the leading of God and to take responsibility for your decisions and actions means everything to your organization and ministry.

You need to be the Global Leader people trust. They need to see a confidence in you that is God-given because you know who He is and that He is with you always.

Boldness is not pride or being a know-it-all. It is not ignoring others and following only your own ideas. It is seeking the truth and direction from God and others and then having the courage to move ahead.

Boldness is confidence. Boldness is courage. Boldness is a willingness to stand alone if necessary.

A Lesson From The Word

Here are the instructions God gave Joshua when he became the leader of the Children of Israel:

Joshua 1:5-10 (NIV) "No one will be able to stand up against you all the days of your life. As I was with Moses, so I will be with you; I will never leave you nor forsake you. Be strong and courageous, because you will lead these people to inherit the land I swore to their forefathers to give them. Be strong and very courageous. Be careful to obey all the law my servant Moses gave you; do not turn from it to the right or to the left, that you may be successful wherever you go. Do not let this Book of the Law depart from your mouth; meditate on it day and night, so that you may be careful to do everything written in it. Then you will be prosperous and successful. Have I not commanded you? Be strong and courageous. Do not be terrified; do not be discouraged, for the LORD your God will be with you wherever you go."

Look at the list of what courage, boldness, and obedience, which seem to be woven together, bring to the leader.

Boldness brings God's presence as well as prosperity and success as a leader.

Boldness also protects the leader from discouragement and fear.

Boldness also allows us to claim God's promises.

How Boldness Will Affect
The Global Leader

People are looking for Global Leaders who know who they are, who know why they are in leadership, and who know where they are going and why. Those are the leaders people want to follow.

A Global Leader who has a boldness, a confidence, and a courage in his leadership style will be followed; he must be very sure that he is following God and not his own ideas.

This will require time with God. In fact, maybe the reputation should be: "He has been with God, that's why he is so bold."

They said that of Moses, they said that of Joshua. They saw that in Peter and John, (Acts 4:13) ordinary men who were bold. As a result, the officials of the day were astonished and knew that "they had been with Jesus."

If we are truly servants of God, building His Kingdom, we will need to be bold to face the discouragements and fears that we will deal with on a daily bases. We dare not give up.

Boldness is contagious. Those who work with you will gain their boldness from you.

Boldness is attractive. People will want to be around you because you have an air of confidence in God that others seek.

Boldness is a choice. Choose to trust God, not yourself.

Action Steps

1. Choose from where you will get your strength.
Will it come from your own skills and abilities? Or will it come from your confidence and trust in God? I have often said that my greatest strength is my confidence in God. What is your greatest strength? The answer will help you decide where your boldness is focused.

2. Ask God to show you where your fears are and ask Him to help you give those areas of fear to Him.
Fear will always try to stop you from moving ahead. Find out where your fears are and give those areas to God so you can be free to trust God through the tough times.

3. Learn to move ahead, trust God, and do your best while trusting God to do all the rest.
A Global Leader has to act when action is necessary. He may not know all the answers, or be able to see the whole picture, but he must act on what he does know

and then trust God for all the rest. He must also be able to correct his direction without pride or fear because what he is doing is building the Kingdom of God under God's direction.

Building God's Kingdom or building your own—that's the choice the Global Leader has to make.

Leadership Demands
CHARACTER

"God, I want to be a Global Leader with character. Give me the courage to pursue that quality." Why are some leaders so connected with their followers?

Why do some leaders have such cooperation and fellowship with those whom they serve?

What is the leadership quality that inspires such honesty, trust, and openness?

People are not impressed by leaders who have façades for different situations or use manipulation to get their way. They are not impressed by leaders who suppress the facts or enhance the truth for personal gain.

People are looking for leaders they can trust, leaders with character. In fact, some would argue that personal character is the most important quality of leadership.

Leadership demands CHARACTER.

What are you like when no one is looking?

Words that would describe the kind of character a Global Christian Leader needs might include: Godliness, righteousness, and Christ-likeness.

The leader with character would constantly be asking two important questions: "What would Jesus do?" and "What would Jesus not do?"

A Lesson From The Word

Proverbs 2:1-11 (NIV) "My son, if you accept my words and store up my commands within you, turning your ear to wisdom and applying your heart to understanding, and if you call out for insight and cry aloud for understanding, and if you look for it as for silver and search for it as for hidden treasure, then you will understand the fear of the LORD and find the knowledge of God. For the LORD gives wisdom, and from his mouth come knowledge and understanding. He holds victory in store for the upright, he is a shield to those whose walk is blameless, for he guards the course of the just and protects the way of his faithful ones. Then you will understand what is right and just and fair—every good path. For wisdom will enter your heart, and knowledge will be pleasant to your soul. Discretion will protect you, and understanding will guard you.

Circle the words that are included in a person's character.

What is the difference between: Fear of the Lord and the Knowledge of God?

What is the difference between: wisdom, knowledge, and understanding?

How can we walk blamelessly?

How The Quality Of Character Will Affect The Global Leader

Trust is a major component of the Global Leader. It affects all of his relationships.

Fellow workers need to be able to trust their leaders' decisions and directions to be in the best interest of the organizational purpose.

Outside partner ministries need to know that there is no spirit of competition or seeking of personal glory from the leader of the other organization. There has to be trust at all times because the enemy is anxious to destroy any cooperation in ministry.

Donors need to be able to trust the leader in his reports, to do what he says he will do.

Humility is another important quality of character. Leadership is a trust, a privilege. We never earn the "right" to lead. It is a privilege entrusted to us by the followers.

If the followers don't follow, we cannot lead. We can only lead when we earn the right to lead.

Honesty with ourselves and with those we work with is the third leg that character stands on. There are a lot of things we don't know and there is nothing wrong with admitting that and working together with the followers to find a solution.

The Global Leader without character will find himself alone and ineffective as he tries to get the job done for personal gain.

Action Steps

1. Get His Word and commands "within you" (:1)

If we don't have God's Word within our lives, we will not have His command either. And if we don't have His commands, we won't have His promises. So how are you doing with getting the Word of God inside your life? Are you putting His Word in your heart so you won't sin against Him? Try memorizing one verse this next week. Start there!

2. Choose "every good path" (:9)

This is a daily decision and commitment…to choose the good path. There are lots of opportunities out there to mess up and sink a ministry. Between "pride" and "fear" we have choices in every opportunity. Be on your guard at all times. Just because it looks good does not mean it is good.

3. Let God "protect and guard" you (:11)

Don't think you can do this on your own. Have patience

to wait on the Lord and let Him be your guide and your guard. Ask for prayer. Ask for wisdom. Ask for help.

Leaders Must Be
DETERMINED

Determination is defined as a "firmness of purpose" or a "fixed purpose."

Determination is fleshed out every day as we make decisions, as we set a course of action, and as we lead others.

When we're not determined, we wonder.
When we're not determined, we get distracted.
When we're not determined, we don't finish well.
When we're not determined, we tire easily.
When we're not determined, we can't see clearly.
When we're not determined, we forget.

Determination is tied to your personal purpose, to your objectives, and to your plan.

Have you ever wanted something so bad that it's all you can think about? Sometimes we fill our lives with so many things that take us away from what we really should be focusing on. Sometimes we chase so many things that we never really accomplish anything.

A leader must be determined.
A leader must be focused on the bigger picture.
A leader must be able to discern what the most important thing is.

Are you determined?

A Lesson From The Word: Peter & Jesus

Matthew 14:25-32 (NIV)

During the fourth watch of the night Jesus went out to them, walking on the lake. When the disciples saw him walking on the lake, they were terrified. "It's a ghost," they said, and cried out in fear. But Jesus immediately said to them: "Take courage! It is I. Don't be afraid." "Lord, if it's you," Peter replied, "tell me to come to you on the water." "Come," he said. Then Peter got down out of the boat, walked on the water and came toward Jesus. But when he saw the wind, he was afraid and, beginning to sink, cried out, "Lord, save me!" Immediately Jesus reached out his hand and caught him. "You of little faith," he said, "why did you doubt?" And when they climbed into the boat, the wind died down. Then those who were in the boat worshiped him, saying, "Truly you are the Son of God."

Peter, in the midst of fear and doubt, wanted to be with Jesus so much that he climbed over the railing of the boat and walked on the water to get to Jesus.

At first, his eyes were fixed on Jesus, his target, and his goal.

Then he took his eyes off of him and began to sink.

Peter demonstrates the power of determination. When you know what you want and what you must do, it drives you to do things you never imagined.

How Being Determined Will Affect The Global Leader

When we talk about determination in a "global" context, you know the pressures that we face.

Have you ever heard these things said to you?
- That's not how we do it anymore.
- There's a new process.
- Wait over there.
- We can't do that in this office.
- Hurry up!
- Please bring more copies.
- You're missing this form.
- We've never done that before.
- Come back tomorrow.
- How much is this worth to you?

Nothing is easy. Everything changes. The rules change.

A Global Leader needs to learn to be determined; otherwise nothing will be accomplished. You are facing obstacles that others will never face. If you know where you're going and you know why you're headed in that direction, then nothing can keep you from accomplishing the task before you.

Don't quit! Don't give up!

Action Steps

1. Know where you're going!

If you want to get moving, you have to know where you're going! You need to determine the course and map the course to get there. Your ability to accomplish the task is based on your ability to figure out where you're going. Don't get lost without a map!

2. Know why you're going there!

It's one thing to know where you're going, it's another to know WHY! This is directly tied to your purpose and your direction. Determining the WHY will make the journey clearer. If you can't answer this question, then go back to step #1.

3. Know who's going with you!

Sometimes the journey is just for us. Sometimes, as leaders, we take others with us. Know who's on board with the "where" and the "why," then take them with you! Two or three are much better than one. You can help each other, you can encourage each other, you can journey together.

Leaders Must Be
ENGAGED

We define the word "engaged" as being "involved."

Leaders can lead without being fully "engaged." An engaged leader is someone who sees the whole situation.

An engaged leader doesn't stop thinking about an issue or a crisis because the workday is over.

An engaged leader believes so strongly in what they're investing their time in that they live it, breathe it, care deeply about it, and don't "disengage" from it.

There is a balance here. I'm not talking about an unhealthy obsession with your ministry or with a project. I'm talking about a full commitment to what you've been called to do.

There are a lot of leaders who get by doing things halfway.

If what we're called to is important, than we need to give it our best, our full attention, our greatest energy.

If you have a hard time engaging and you don't understand why, then you need to step back and figure it out.

Genuine "engagement" happens when you're involved, when you really care about what's happening, and when you can't get it off of your mind! Otherwise, it will pass!

A Lesson From The Word: Gideon

Judges 7: 1-25 (NIV)

7:2,3 The Lord said to Gideon, "You have too many men for me to deliver Midian into their hands. In order that Israel may not boast against me that her own strength has saved her, announce now to the people, 'Anyone who trembles with fear may turn back and leave Mount Gilead.'" So twenty-two thousand men left, while ten thousand remained.

7:4 But the Lord said to Gideon, "There are still too many men. Take them down to the water, and I will sift them for you there. If I say, 'This one shall go with you.' He shall go; but if I say, 'This one shall not go with you,' he shall not go."

7:5-7 So Gideon took the men down to the water. There the Lord told him, "Separate those who lap the water with their tongues like a dog from those who kneel down to drink." Three hundred men lapped with their hands to their mouths. All the rest got down on their knees to drink. The Lord said to Gideon, "With the three hundred men that lapped I will save you and give the Midianites into your hands. Let all the other men go, each to his own place."

God wanted Gideon to know He was God!

Gideon fully trusted God and believed in what God was going to do in him and through him.

Gideon was "engaged" in his relationship with God… "All In," "Fully Committed," "Willing," "Hanging In There."

How Being Able To Engage Will Affect The Global Leader

Global Leaders face so many distractions. There are demands, opportunities, requests, and wonderful things happening all around you.

Sometimes people push their expectations on you, thinking that you will jump at any opportunity.

The word that has helped me over the years is the word "alignment." Alignment is simply keeping things in order, or keeping things "straight."

For a Global Leader, the questions you need to ask when given a new opportunity are these:
- Does this fit with my purpose, my passion?
- Does this build His kingdom or my kingdom?
- Does this opportunity fit with our organization's plan?

Alignment is simply keeping on task.

When you keep on task with what you've been called and given to do, you will be able to engage.

Don't you want to spend your time doing exactly what God created you to do? When you follow Him, it's easy to engage with everything you've got!

Action Steps

1. Ask God to show you where you need to spend your time, energy, and passion.

This is critical! Learn to discern God's plan for your life and your ministry, then trust Him! If you know, believe, and trust that your call is from God, you will be able to fully engage in all He has for you.

2. Learn to say "NO."

Other people's opportunities aren't necessarily YOUR opportunities. Sometimes you have to say NO in order to fully engage in what you should be focusing on. When there's too much on your plate, you aren't able to do anything effectively.

3. When you know where you're going, be ALL there!

There's freedom that comes when things are clear and when we're able to fully focus on the task at hand. This doesn't mean that it's easy, but it helps us to know where to focus, where to apply our energy, and what we should be spending our time doing. Once you determine that, DO IT! Be all there!

Leaders Must Be
FLEXIBLE

Leaders either praise flexibility or curse it! There are times that flexibility isn't an option! Sometimes what needs to be done, NEEDS TO BE DONE!

Flexibility can also be a gift.

Do you know people who don't get rattled when life throws a challenge at them? How would you respond to that challenge?

The ability to be flexible will also enable you as a leader not to panic when the unexpected hits you. Being flexible will help you stay calm, it will help you stay focused, and it will help you keep your eye on the end goal, no matter what it takes to get there.

Flexibility is a term that is often used when people don't plan or prepare correctly. That's not what we're talking about. That's called "bad leadership."

Flexibility is needed when there's a clear plan and process in place and circumstances keep you from fulfilling that plan, forcing you to try another route.

Often the best planning and preparation will be destroyed by some new challenge.

Don't give up! Look at it from a new perspective and keep moving forward!

A Lesson From The Word: Joseph

Genesis 37-46

The story of Joseph is an epic tale of deceit, jealousy, hatred, suffering, and disappointment.

Joseph is sold into slavery by his brothers.

Joseph is wrongly accused and imprisoned because he said no to Potiphar's wife.

Joseph is freed from prison because of his ability to interpret dreams.

Joseph is given great responsibility by the Pharaoh of Egypt.

The story of Joseph is also a story of faithfulness, perseverance, integrity, and forgiveness.

Read the whole story and think about Joseph's life as a young shepherd, with his whole life before him. Think about how his plans were changed when his brothers turned on him, and then think about his statement in Genesis 45:5 (NIV) as he speaks to his brothers: "And now, do not be distressed and do not be angry with yourselves for selling me here, because it was to save lives that God sent me ahead of you."

Do you believe that God really has a plan? Are you willing to trust Him with that? Are you willing to be flexible and possibly change your plans in order to be obedient to Him?

How Being Flexible Will Affect The Global Leader

Global Leaders face challenges that others don't often face:
- A government coup
- A riot or manifestation
- A bank closure
- A lack of power or utilities
- No fuel for your vehicle
- No internet or e-mail

I could go on and on, but these are real issues that you face. All leaders face issues, but flexibility is essential for you to survive in the world that God has placed you in.

Learning to be flexible will help you to be a better leader. Others are watching how you handle tough situations, how you respond to crisis, and what your attitude is when your plans are thrown out.

The world responds in anger, in panic, in desperation. You need to respond rationally, with hope and determination.

Remember, God is in control. Flexibility is not a cure for bad planning.

Flexibility is a gift to help you navigate a world that is uncertain, ever changing, and in crisis!

Action Steps

1. Plan your agenda and schedule with some margins.
Most of the time, we pack our lives with too much stuff to do! Learn to create some space in your schedule so that when the unplanned things hit you, it doesn't destroy you. Create some space and when there aren't unexpected things there, use the time wisely!

2. Learn to determine God's plan vs. Man's distractions.
Flexibility doesn't mean that we allow anything and everything to get in the way. You still need to determine what God has for you and what a simple distraction is. Learn to discern the difference! Flexibility is important when God throws a curve at you or when He wants you to do something else, not just when you get bored or uninterested.

3. Look for the best in bad situations!

When you face something unexpected, don't spend all of your time whining and grumbling about it. Look for the best in the situation that you've been given. Sometimes the thing God is trying to teach us comes from the journey, not from the end task.

Leaders Must Be
GENUINE

No one wants to work for someone who is a phony. That would be someone who is one thing to this group and something else to the next group and, perhaps, even something else to the next group…a hypocrite…a fake!

No one can trust a leader who says what he thinks the people want to hear even though he doesn't believe or agree with it.

No one wants a leader who will do anything or say anything to get what he wants. No one wants a leader who doesn't mean what he says.

No one will follow a man who changes with the winds of opportunity and does not have a solid purpose or consistent values.

People want to know that their leaders have values that do not change, that they have commitments they mean to keep, that they have a purpose that is their guide.

People want leaders who are genuine. "What you see is what you get" kind of stuff. No hidden agendas. No secret motives.

Openness and honesty are two very important traits in a leader.

No one can be perfect. We all have strengths and weaknesses. Openness and honesty help us surround ourselves with people who can help us in those areas of weakness.

A Lesson From The Word: Timothy

1 Timothy 4:1-16 (NLT)

:1-2 Now the Holy Spirit tells us clearly that in the last times some will turn away from the true faith; they will follow deceptive spirits and teachings that come from demons. These people are hypocrites and liars, and their consciences are dead.

:6-9 If you explain these things to the brothers and sisters, Timothy, you will be a worthy servant of Christ Jesus, one who is nourished by the message of faith and the good teaching you have followed. Do not waste time arguing over godless ideas and old wives' tales. Instead, train yourself to be godly. "Physical training is good, but training for godliness is much better, promising benefits in this life and in the life to come." This is a trustworthy saying, and everyone should accept it.

:12-16 Don't let anyone think less of you because you are young. Be an example to all believers in what you say, in the way you live, in your love, your faith, and your purity. Until I get there, focus on reading the Scriptures to the church, encouraging the believers, and teaching them. Do not neglect the spiritual gift you received through the prophecy spoken over you when the elders of the church laid their hands on you. Give your complete attention to these matters. Throw yourself into your tasks so that everyone will see your progress. Keep a close watch on how you live and on your teaching. Stay true to what is right for the sake of your own salvation and the salvation of those who hear you.

How Being Genuine Will Affect The Global Leader

A Global Leader has to be a man of his word. People have to believe him and trust him to say what he means and mean what he says.

In fact, a Global Leader has to work extra hard to clarify things so that everyone is on the same page and has the same understanding.

Working with cultural differences is hard, but the Global Leader has to go a step further so there is never any doubt of understanding between him and his fellow workers or partners.

Sometimes the only understanding we have between different people is the understanding that we can trust the other person to do what is best for us, for the ministry, and for the partner. That trust is based on how much we know about the other person. How much we know about the other person is based on how open the other person has been with us. Openness is the root of being genuine.

The Global Leader has to be a man of his word, with honest actions and motives and an openness about his strengths and weaknesses. He has to be a real person with feelings and concerns.

There is no room for superstars with no human concerns or feelings in Global Leadership. We are working with people. People have concerns. We must share those concerns.

Action Steps

1. Keep your conscience alive.
Never get to the position where you think you know it all or where you think you are beyond the reach of the enemy. Always guard your mind and the things you put into it. Keep your conscience clean.

2. Be a worthy servant and train yourself to be Godly!
Now, there is a full-time lifestyle. View yourself as a servant, not as the boss. Serving God, serving your staff, serving others. Work hard to serve others. Then focus on the Godly life. What can I do to be more like Jesus? If you don't want to be a leader who looks like Jesus, do something else!

3. Work at being an example to all believers in five areas:

(1) What you say

(2) The way you live

(3) In your love

(4) In your faith

(5) In your purity

Leaders Must Be
HUMBLE

The main goal for godly leaders is to reflect the life of Christ in their own lives.

How do we do that without admitting that we are nothing except what God has allowed us to be and that we have no skills except what God has given to us?

Jesus said He came to serve! When He came, He took the form of a servant. He did not flaunt his position or power. He knew He was sent for a purpose and He stayed true to that purpose.

There is a reason God has allowed you to be a leader. You have a choice: operate on your own agenda with pride and arrogance, or give yourself to His plan, accept His leadership, and don't act like it is all your idea.

No one wants to follow a leader who seeks the praise and the attention, who claims all success as his own. People want to be a part of a team. They want to be recognized by the leader for work well done.

The hard part is that you cannot seek to be humble. You cannot claim humility, or talk about how humble you are.

Humility comes when you recognize Christ as the head of your life and yield to His plan and control. Humility is a gift from God in exchange for your surrender to Him. Humility is letting God get all the credit, which is right, because nothing happens without His involvement.

A Lesson From The Word: Jesus

Philippians 2:1-11 (NIV)

If you have any encouragement from being united with Christ, if any comfort from his love, if any fellowship with the Spirit, if any tenderness and compassion, then make my joy complete by being like-minded, having the same love, being one in spirit and purpose. Do nothing out of selfish ambition or vain conceit, but in humility consider others better than yourselves. Each of you should look not only to your own interests, but also to the interests of others. Your attitude should be the same as that of Christ Jesus: Who, being in very nature God, did not consider equality with God something to be grasped, but made himself nothing, taking the very nature of a servant, being made in human likeness. And being found in appearance as a man, he humbled himself and became obedient to death—even death on a cross! Therefore God exalted him to the highest place and gave him the name that is above every name, that at the name of Jesus every knee should bow, in heaven and on earth and under the earth, and every tongue confess that Jesus Christ is Lord, to the glory of God the Father.

We often get things mixed up. We spend our life trying to exalt ourselves and God has to work to humble us.

It has to be the other way around. Like Jesus, we need to humble ourselves, committing our leadership to His way and plan, and let Him exalt us if and when He wants.

How Being Humble Will Affect The Global Leader

This quality will define your leadership. It will set in place how you will treat others, what your major focus will be, and how you will be seen in your role.

The Global Leader in Christian ministry, doing God's work and doing it in his own strength and skills, will greatly limit the success and usefulness of the ministry.

The Global Leader in Christian ministry, doing God's work and doing it without drawing attention to himself, will be amazed by what God will be able to accomplish through his humble heart and spirit.

Someone has said, "It is amazing what can be accomplished when you don't care who gets the credit!"

The Global Leader who can minister without getting the credit or having his name mentioned will draw other ministries for strategic partnerships. The commitment has to be to build the Kingdom of God, not our own kingdom.

The attitude and humility of the Global Leader will form the personality and reputation of the organization. A humble leader builds a humble, serving organization. A proud leader builds a proud, self-centered organization.

Action Steps

1. Admit you are His servant and pray to do things His way. That would mean you yield yourself to Christ and let Him get all the glory for anything you do. That also means you focus on being as much like Him as you possibly can. You are serious about asking the question, "What would Jesus do?" as well as "What would Jesus not do?"

2. Keep your head and remember you can do nothing in His Kingdom without His involvement. Paul meant it when he told the church of Philippi (4:13), "I can do all things through Christ who is my strength." He wasn't talking about himself; he was talking about Christ. After all he had done, he recognized that he was nothing and Christ was everything.

3. Focus on the fact that He put you where you are and has given you the opportunity of leadership. Spend the rest of your life thanking Him by putting Him first and always giving Him the credit and glory for anything you do.

Leaders Must Have
INTEGRITY

I recently heard the story of another leader who had fallen. I'm so tired of hearing these stories! People are hurt, families are torn apart, and all of the things that were taught, modeled, and encouraged are thrown out.

It keeps happening over and over again.

I don't think we have to be perfect. We have a God who forgives, who restores, and who is filled with grace. However, some of us live our lives asking for forgiveness, instead of trying to do things right!

Leaders' impact, effectiveness, and legacy all come back to how they live their lives, how they conduct the business of ministry, and how they lead and treat others.

It's really simple: DO THE RIGHT THING!

God's word teaches us.
Our nation's laws give us parameters.
The church guides us.

Why do some leaders continue to think that they know what's best?

Don't try to play the game. Don't walk the line!

A Lesson From The Word: Samuel

1 Samuel 12:1-4 (NIV)

Samuel said to all Israel, "I have listened to everything you said to me and have set a king over you. Now you have a king as your leader. As for me, I am old and gray, and my sons are here with you. I have been your leader from my youth until this day. Here I stand. Testify against me in the presence of the Lord and his anointed. Whose ox have I taken? Whose donkey have I taken? Whom have I cheated? Whom have I oppressed? From whose hand have I accepted a bribe to make me shut my eyes? If I have done any of these, I will make it right."

"You have not cheated or oppressed us," they replied. "You have not taken anything from anyone's hand."

"He is witness," they said.

Imagine this…

You're saying goodbye to the people you've lead for years and as part of your "farewell speech," you open the floor and challenge people to testify concerning how you lived as a leader.

Amazing! Pretty risky, too?

Is that how you want to live your life? What other way is there?

How Having Integrity Will Affect The Global Leader

Maybe the better question is this: "How will lack of integrity affect the Global Leader?"

How we live our life affects everything: our families, our teams, our ministries, our relationships, our word.

Global Leaders must build trust in order to be effective in their ministry, their call, and their impact. When we compromise ourselves, it trickles down to everyone around us.

We live in a world that has marginalized integrity. There is no absolute truth, and there is always a way around the law or the rules.

We are faced everyday with a response to that lack of integrity, and how we respond and react has a direct correlation to the effectiveness of our ministry and our lives.

There is truth. There is the "right" way to do things. Sometimes it's more difficult, but it's right!

Are you willing to live that way?

Are you willing to model integrity in everything you do?

Action Steps

1. Put some people around you. One of the best ways to proactively keep on track is to surround yourself with people who will ask you the "hard" questions. People you trust, people you respect, and people you'll listen to. You need people in your life who will speak truth, even when it's painful!

2. Ask God for help, daily! Our power, our discipline, our desire comes from Him! Ask Him daily to help you make good decisions. Ask Him daily for protection. Ask Him daily for the strength to walk in integrity! Remember, in 1 Peter 5:8 we're told to "be self-controlled and alert. Your enemy the devil prowls around like a roaring lion looking for someone to devour. Resist him, standing firm in the faith…"

3. You're not alone! You not only need people to hold you accountable, but you need to help others to walk with integrity! We really do need each other!

Leaders Must Be JOYFUL

Being joyful is not simply being "happy." Joy is deeper than happiness. Joy is "relishing the happiness." It's deeper.

Sometimes as leaders, we try to put on a happy face, even when things aren't going so well.

Being joyful means that even when we're dealing with crisis or when we're in the midst of a tough situation, we find joy in:

- The place God has placed us
- The people we get to serve and work with
- The opportunity to learn and grow
- The big picture and the end result

Do you ever wake up in the morning feeling glad to be alive?

You may be tired, you may not have slept enough, but there's a sense of JOY that you have to get up, get moving, and make an impact today.

That's joy.

I believe we have a choice in how we respond and how we react.

Leaders don't have to be happy all the time, but we do need to find joy in all that we're doing and all that we're entrusted with!

A Lesson From The Word: Joyful

Joy is spoken of throughout the Bible, and we're reminded over and over again to have "joy" in our lives.

The story in Matthew 13:44 tells the parable of the man who found a treasure in a field, and in his "joy" went and sold all that he had to buy the field. This is a story talking about the kingdom of heaven.

The story in Matthew 28:8 tells us of Mary Magdalene and the other Mary's encounter with the angel after Jesus' resurrection. We're told that they were "afraid, yet filled with joy."

Joy is an interesting emotion and it's an interesting response!

Sometimes we feel that we can't control this emotion, yet in Galatians 5, we're reminded that joy is one of the fruits of the Spirit and is evidence of Christ working in and through our lives.

We're reminded:
"The joy of the Lord is your strength." Nehemiah 8:10

"Let us fix our eyes on Jesus, the author and perfecter of our faith, who for the joy set before him endured the cross, scorning its shame, and sat down at the right hand of the throne of God." Hebrews 12:2

"Be joyful always; pray continually; give thanks in all circumstances, for this is God's will for you in Christ Jesus." 1 Thessalonians 5:16-18

How Being Joyful Will Affect The Global Leader

There are so many things that "steal our joy." We allow these things into our lives and then we complain because life just isn't fun anymore! Some of these things might be:
- Being too busy to enjoy what we're doing
- Allowing others' criticism to take root in our lives, affecting the way we lead
- Not spending any time doing things we like to do
- Jumping from one crisis to another, continually
- Focusing on ourselves and our needs instead of others
- Making bad decisions that affect us for a long time

Our world is full of people who have either forgotten what joy is really all about or who have never experienced real joy. Our job is to be joyful!
- When we're driving a car in traffic
- When we're standing in line

- When people are being rude to us
- When our team fails us
- When things don't make sense

Our first reaction should be JOY! Not anger, not fear, not resentment, not bitterness, not sorrow...JOY!

Action Steps

1. Choose Joy.

We all have a choice in how we react to situations and circumstances. Often it comes in a split-second decision. Make the decision today to "choose joy." Don't let a lousy situation determine your response. We have enough grumblers and complainers.

2. Be Contagious!

Let your genuine joy spread to others. It's amazing how a joyful attitude can be used to completely transform others around you. Don't hide your joy, show it in your response, in your attitude, and in your actions. Let others see it!

3. Let it come from your Heart!

It's one thing to "show joy." We can all fake it. We can smile or laugh or respond positively in light of a tough situation. I want to encourage you to allow the joy to flow from your heart; this means that it's "real" joy. Joy is given to us by the Spirit. Recognize where our joy comes from! As this joy comes from our heart, it will spread to our faces, and others will recognize the real joy we have.

Leaders Must Be
KIND

Kindness and forgiveness are brothers in the Christian faith.

Paul told us to "be kind and compassionate to one another, forgiving each other, just as in Christ God forgave you." Ephesians 4:32

Kindness is when I do not expect the other person to be perfect.

Kindness is when I hold judgment until all the facts, both sides of the story, are in.

Kindness is giving forgiveness, not judgment.

Kindness is what God gives us and what we should give to one another without reservation, without conditions.

The leader who is kind understands other people. They see their own weaknesses and can forgive the same in others.

Kindness and gentleness are also related. Treat people with gentleness and kindness will follow.

If we are going to model our leadership style after Jesus, than we must practice kindness…just as in Christ, God has been kind to us.

A Lesson From The Word: Barnabas

One of the reasons Paul was so successful in building the church in Asia and Europe was because of the kindness Barnabas showed toward him.

When Paul tried to join the disciples in Jerusalem (Acts 9:27) and they were afraid of him because of his reputation, it was Barnabas who said, "It's OK. He's with me."

When Barnabas saw the growing church in Antioch, he went to Tarsus, found Paul, and brought him back to help him build the church (Acts 11:25).

When Barnabas was sent by the church to Judea with a gift to meet their need, he took Paul with him so the church could meet him (Acts 11:30).

And when John Mark left in the middle of the first missionary journey (Acts 13:13), it was Barnabas who gave John Mark a second chance (Acts 15:39).

Barnabas practiced kindness in his relationships with others, whether powerful preachers like Paul, with large reputations or young men, like John Mark, just learning their way.

Barnabas is a good model for us.

How Being Kind Will Affect The Global Leader

Isaiah (63:7) tells us well of the role kindness plays in the life of a Global Leader:

I will tell of the kindnesses of the Lord, the deeds for which he is to be praised, according to all the Lord has done for us. Yes, the many good things He has done for the house of Israel, according to His compassion and many kindnesses. Surely, they are my people…

A Global Leader has to remember the kindnesses given to him on his journey of life. As he remembers what others have shown him, he has to pass those along to others as well.

A Global Leader has to testify aloud of the kindnesses that others have shown him. In the expression of those acts of kindness, he will remind himself to do the same as well as encourage others to extend kindness.

A Global Leader who is kind will be followed. He will be copied. He will be appreciated.

Kindness is what people see as they compare us to the life of Christ. Gentleness, kindness, forgiveness are three words that have to be a part of the Global Leader's style of leadership.

Action Steps

1. Proverbs 12:25 "An anxious heart weighs a man down, but a kind word cheers him up!" This is where we start. Develop the habit of saying a kind word to another person everyday. Look for ways to express your appreciation. Look for areas of growth or a job well done. Don't let a day go by without saying something kind to another person.

2. I Corinthians 13:4 "Love is patient. Love is kind." It seems love, patience, and kindness have a connection to each other. So when you are tempted to feel impatient with someone, let that be a signal that instead of impatience, you will express kindness to them. Make that a habit…when you feel impatient, count to ten and think of something kind to say.

3. I Thessalonians 5:15 "Always try to be kind to each other and to everyone else." Sometimes it is the people we know best, or the people we work with, or family members to whom we fail to show kindness. We assume they will understand our frustration or harsh words or impatience or unforgiveness. Those closest to us need to see our kindness as well. Start there. When you blow it, quickly ask their forgiveness. Let them know how you value them. Everyday thank God for His kindness and forgiveness!

Leaders Must Be
LOVING

Sometimes leaders get caught up in the mechanics of leadership: We know what we should do, how we should lead, where we need to go.

Sometimes leadership is all about getting through our list, accomplishing our goals, and being able to measure growth and impact.

Sometimes we have to stop and consider that there are things much more important then our agenda.

Jesus reminds us that the "greatest" thing, the most important thing is to love Him and love others.

How do we do that as an effective leader? How does this affect the way we lead, the way we treat people, the direction we're going?

Sometimes getting someplace is not nearly as important as the journey it takes to get there.

- Don't run over people; love them.
- Don't get so busy that you forget about the people who are coming with you.
- Don't ignore the reason you're in leadership…

It's Him!

A Lesson From The Word:
The Greatest Commandment

Matthew 22:34-39 (NIV)

Hearing that Jesus had silenced the Sadducees, the Pharisees got together. One of them, an expert in the law, tested him with this question: "Teacher, which is the greatest commandment in the Law?"

Jesus replied: "'Love the Lord your God with all your heart and with all your soul and with all your mind.' This is the first and greatest commandment. And the second is like it: 'Love your neighbor as yourself.' All the Law and the Prophets hang on these two commandments."

When I think of Jesus' commandment to us all in Matthew, I'm reminded that what He wants from us is LOVE. He's calling us to love Him with everything we've got, and to also love those around us.

The root of these two commandments comes from the Old Testament.

In Deuteronomy 6:4-6, we're told: "Hear, O Israel: The Lord our God, the Lord is one. Love the Lord your God with all your heart and with all your soul and with all your strength. These commandments that I give you today are to be upon your hearts."

In Leviticus 19:18, we're told: "Do not seek revenge or bear a grudge against one of your people, but love your neighbor as yourself. I am the Lord."

How Being Loving Will Affect The Global Leader

Global Leaders must learn to rely first and foremost on Him. He will give you the strength, the wisdom, the ability to do everything if you put your faith, your trust, and your relationship in Him first!

There's no compromise here…He calls us to love Him first with everything we've got, then out of that relationship, He uses us to love others.

What's the goal of your ministry or organization?

What's the end product?

What's the purpose of your life as a follower of Him?

If it's not about loving Him and loving others, I challenge you to go back to the Word and look at Christ's commandment to all of us.

Don't make it so complicated that you forget what we're doing this for.

Leadership, vision, strategy, innovation, and direction are critical, but we grow in those things so that we can fulfill His call on our lives...

And simply, that's to LOVE!

Action Steps

The question here is, "How do I do this?"

1. Spend time with Him.
It's hard to fall in love with someone that you don't spend time with. Spend time with God. Listen to Him. Talk to Him. Read His Word. Serve Him. Follow Him. A relationship is built by an investment of time. Make this a priority in your life!

2. Open your eyes to the world around you.
Everyday we move through life either with our eyes closed or our eyes focused on the things we're doing. Take some time to see what's going on around you. You'll be amazed at the opportunities and the needs that jump out at you when you're looking for them. Learn to live with your eyes wide open!

3. Lead in love, even when you don't feel like it!
Jesus tells us that when we love Him and when we love others, then we're doing exactly what he's created us to do. As a leader, don't just be loving in private, but allow

that to be seen by those around you. Model this, teach this, show others that you are committed to Jesus and his commandments.

Leaders Must Be
MULTIPLIERS

I don't know about you, but sometimes I'm overwhelmed by the task the Lord gave us to "tell the world!"

Sometimes I think that I'm the one that has to do everything!

If we want to make the biggest impact, we have to learn to:
- Work with others
- Empower others
- Teach and share all that we know
- Delegate others
- Enable others

We also need to be able to learn from others!

If we're serious about effective ministry, our ability to multiply into others will determine our success and our effectiveness.

The day of working on our own is over: strategic partnerships, effective teams, and joint ventures are the buzz today.

What's the most important thing you know?

Are you willing to share that with someone else or are you completely happy and content to do your own thing?

A Lesson From The Word: Timothy

2 Timothy 2:2 (NIV)

"And the things you have heard me say in the presence of many witnesses entrust to reliable men who will also be qualified to teach others."

Paul is writing to Timothy from prison. He's suffering physically and emotionally, and he's feeling abandoned and hopeless.

At this time in his life, he's thinking of the most important lessons he can pass onto his disciple, Timothy, lessons that Timothy will take and share with others. Paul is locked up! He has to rely on Timothy and others to continue spreading the Good News!

2 Timothy 2:2 summarizes one of our roles as leaders, and that is our ability to teach others so they can teach others!

What a legacy Paul leaves to Timothy, and what a legacy Timothy leaves to the early church: Multiplication!

Do you like to do it all yourself?

What would happen if you were incapacitated, locked-up, taken out of the game…Who would step in to carry on the things that you've given your life for?

How Being A Multiplier Will Affect The Global Leader

Sometimes it's difficult to find qualified people who you can pour into and multiply into.

I think one of the most important challenges for a Global Leader is the task of identifying potential leaders. Sometimes we're looking for people who have experience, natural skills, and a desire to jump in! It's always easier when you have these kinds of people lined up, waiting to get involved.

In the world we live in, these people are hard to find, so we have to look for people who have "potential." Identifying potential leaders might start by:
• Finding someone with a compassionate heart
• Identifying someone who shares your vision & passion
• Bringing someone in who has a certain skill set
• Looking for someone with integrity and purpose

Remember, you're not looking for someone just like you! You're looking for someone who will capture your vision and carry it out! Many times, we multiply only into people who are just like us.

Look for leaders who have the potential to be greater than you, to do more than you, to take your vision further and broader. Don't be threatened by them.

Multiply, pour into them, then cheer them on!

Action Steps

1. Surround yourself with people who want to learn!
Leading on your own is often easier: you don't have to wait for others, you can do things the way you like them, and there's no one to complain. However, you can't do it all alone! Learn to surround yourself with people who will learn from you and who will work with you. Build a team! Share your vision and your call, then you'll be able to accomplish so much more!

2. Learn to delegate.
Delegation is not simply telling others how to do things. Delegation is a process of modeling, teaching, supporting, and passing things off. Often we delegate by giving a list of "to do's" to a subordinate. Delegation works when people learn all that we know and we help them to apply it and to achieve success.

3. Find joy in others' growth and success!
A multiplying leader will find great joy in the successes of those who are working around you. Sometimes it's even better than when you did something on your own!

Learn to celebrate in others' successes! It's a great feeling of satisfaction.

Leaders Must
NURTURE

No one wants to serve a leader who only thinks of himself. I want to serve someone who is concerned with my personal growth and development.

A leader who is not helping those who serve with him grow in their skills and abilities is a "user" not a "builder."

A leader is wise if he helps those who serve with him become better at what they do. In that way, the whole ministry will grow and develop.

To "nurture" is to "nourish." To "nourish" is "to provide the food that the staff needs to grow and live."

A leader nourishes by encouraging his fellow workers.

A leader nourishes by making sure his people have the best training available.

A leader nourishes by helping his co-workers when they need help. A leader stands with his workers.

It takes time and desire to nurture.

You cannot be a self-centered, insecure, jealous leader and still try to nurture. You must be willing to give it away, to help your co-worker become like you, maybe even better than you.

A Lesson From The Word

Paul is speaking to the Elders in Ephesus. He knows that he will not see them again and tells them. They weep! Paul tells them how to nurture even as he was nurtured by Barnabas:

Acts 20:25-32 (NLT)

25 And now I know that none of you to whom I have preached the Kingdom will ever see me again.

26 I declare today that I have been faithful. If anyone suffers eternal death, it's not my fault,

27 for I didn't shrink from declaring all that God wants you to know.

28 So guard yourselves and God's people. Feed and shepherd God's flock—his church, purchased with his own blood—over which the Holy Spirit has appointed you as elders.

29 I know that false teachers, like vicious wolves, will come in among you after I leave, not sparing the flock.

30 Even some men from your own group will rise up

and distort the truth in order to draw a following.

31 Watch out! Remember the three years I was with you—my constant watch and care over you night and day, and my many tears for you.

32 And now I entrust you to God and the message of his grace that is able to build you up and give you an inheritance with all those he has set apart for himself.

My question for you is: Could this ever be said about you?

Paul was a nurturer. He wanted to leave a strong church behind after he left. He knew he was leaving. He was ready and he wanted the church ready.

How The Quality Of Nurturing Will Affect The Global Leader

Paul tells Timothy (2 Timothy 2:2) that he needs to surround himself with people with the same passions and commitments that he has, people who care about the future and the next generation.

Then he needs to teach those people what he knows about the Kingdom, the Church, and life itself. He needs to "pass on" what he knows about preaching and teaching the Good News.

So, what about us? Can it be any different?

Have you found those people who can learn what you can teach? People who share your vision? People who share your passion? Have you identified those who will take your place? Paul found Timothy. He poured himself into Timothy. He taught him everything he knew.

He did the same to the Elders from Ephesus. He wanted them ready for the hard times. He wanted them to know how to win the battle they were going to be in.

How are you preparing others? Do you think you will be here forever? Wrong! You must prepare for tomorrow.

Who is on your list to spend time with? Who do you plan to pass your years of experience and knowledge, good and bad, to? It WILL take time!

Action Steps From Verse 28 And 31

1. We are to guard ourselves and to guard God's people.
The enemy wants to destroy the church. He wants to destroy your ministry. He wants to destroy your people. Someone needs to be standing guard over God's people so a warning can be sounded when they see the enemy at work. That is the role of the nurturer!

2. We are to feed and shepherd God's flock.
We are to teach, to train, to lead our co-workers to a place of safety. We are to be trusted by them. We are to care for them. We are to pray for them. We are to be on

the lookout for the growth and development of others.

3. We are to watch out!

Like parents help their children grow, we are to help our coworkers grow. That means we must know them, know their dreams, understand their weaknesses. We are to watch out for them and to warn them when we see danger. We are God's agent to help them be all they can be as they serve and work in the ministry.

A Leader Must Be
OPTIMISTIC

Being optimistic is not being happy. The dictionary defines being optimistic as being "hopeful and confident about the future."

It's difficult to work with optimism today. There are so many negative things around us. So many people without hope for the future. So many things that just keep pulling us down and getting our focus off of what we're supposed to be about.

Are you optimistic?

How do you respond when everything around you seems to be crashing in on you?

How do you show and model optimism to those around you?

Responding with optimism is a choice and it's one that you must make daily. Sometimes it's not easy. Sometimes it may seem impossible. The choice is yours.

Dietrich Bonhoeffer says: "The essence of optimism is that it takes no account of the present, but it is a source of inspiration, of vitality and hope where others have resigned; it enables a man to hold his head high, to claim the future for himself and not to abandon it to his enemy."

A Lesson From The Word

Philippians 4:11-13 (ESV)

Not that I am speaking of being in need, for I have learned in whatever situation I am to be content. I know how to be brought low, and I know how to abound. In any and every circumstance, I have learned the secret of facing plenty and hunger, abundance and need. I can do all things through him who strengthens me.

Paul writes this from prison. He had been there a long time. He had been falsely charged and unjustly treated.

Yet even with these horrible circumstances, Paul writes about the source of his strength, Jesus Christ.

Paul's secret to living amid life's difficulties is simple: trust God.

His message is that sometimes life is really hard. Sometimes you have to go through things that you don't think you'll ever survive. Sometimes you're put in situations where there doesn't appear to be any hope.

In those situations, trust God. He will give you the strength to make it. He will help you to see Him in every circumstance. He will be with you.

Don't give up. Remember where your strength comes from!

How Being Optimistic Will Affect A Global Leader

Every Global Leader faces trials, challenges and situations that may seem to be insurmountable. Many leaders quit when they face this kind of opposition or when these challenges get too tough.

Being optimistic is an attitude that transfers into action.

Your ability to see the possibilities, the potential and the good in things that others can't see will set you apart as a leader. The world is desperately looking for leaders who are "hopeful and confident about the future," even when things are tough.

It seems that the world is a mess: natural disasters, collapsing economies, political corruption, terrorism, war, poverty, oppression, desperation, and on and on.

The world needs leaders who see hope in all things.

The world needs leaders who don't ignore all that's going on around them, but who can lead people through it, helping them to see the positive in everything.

Life is hard, but in the words of Paul, "I can do ALL things through him who strengthens me."

Action Steps

1. Remember.
Take some time to remember who Christ is and what He's already done for you. You have life. You have hope. You have a secure future.

2. Make the choice.
Sometimes, you have to make the conscious choice to be optimistic as opposed to being pessimistic. Choose to see the positive in things. Choose to not be critical. Make that choice daily.

3. Spread optimism.
Don't choose it and keep it to yourself. Spread it around to everyone you come in contact with. Live it, teach it, model it. Let it come through in every conversation you have and in every situation you find yourself in. Be contagiously optimistic!

A Leader Must Have
PURPOSE

What is the intended result you want as you commit your life to be a Global Leader?

What is your goal?
Do you have a goal?
Can you measure how you are doing?
Do you know why you are doing what you are doing?
There is a reason you are doing what you are doing.
That will be your "purpose."

When you discover the "why" for what you are doing, you will know your purpose.

Your purpose will define why you exist and why you are doing what you are doing. If you don't know your purpose, then ask: What you are living for? What is important to you? What could you do that would make your life a success? What do you want people to say about you after you are gone? That will help define your purpose.

People want to follow someone who has a purpose that matches their purpose. Organizations want a leader whose purpose is the same as their purpose. That's when they can work together. That's when things happen.

Your purpose cannot be to "look good," or be "powerful," or be "number one," or "get paid more." Your purpose has to be to "build the Kingdom of God" and to "glorify Christ."

A Lesson From The Word

Esther had purpose. She understood what she wanted to accomplish with her life. She saw why she was living!

Esther 4:13-16 (NLT)

13 Mordecai sent this reply to Esther: "Don't think for a moment that because you're in the palace you will escape when all other Jews are killed.

14 If you keep quiet at a time like this, deliverance and relief for the Jews will arise from some other place, but you and your relatives will die. Who knows if perhaps you were made queen for just such a time as this?"

15 Then Esther sent this reply to Mordecai:

16 "Go and gather together all the Jews of Susa and fast for me. Do not eat or drink for three days, night or day. My maids and I will do the same. And then, though it is against the law, I will go in to see the king. If I must die, I must die."

First, the question by Mordecai: "Who knows if perhaps you were made queen for just such a time as this?" That comes right to the heart of purpose! Do you know what God wants you to do?

Then, Esther's response: "I will go in to see the king. If I must die, I must die." That speaks to the commitment to purpose! Are you willing to do anything in order to do what you know God wants you to do?

How The Quality Of Purpose Will Affect The Global Leader

JESUS, the greatest Global Leader, said, "The thief's purpose is to steal and kill and destroy. My purpose is to give them a rich and satisfying life." John 10:10

MOSES, a Global Leader, talks about God's purpose becoming his purpose as he led the people. Deuteronomy 4:32-40

SOLOMON, a king, says his purpose was to build the temple to God in Jerusalem. I Kings 6:1-8:66

JEHOSHAPHAT was blessed by God as he shares that his passion is to follow God's way! 2 Chronicles 17:1-19

DAVID, another Global Leader, tells what his passion for God causes him to do. Psalm 63

JEREMIAH, a Global Leader, tells us how he endured days of false beliefs in a rebellious nation. Jeremiah 16:19-21

JOHN THE BAPTIST, a Global Leader, knows who he is and why he is here. Mark 1:1-9

PAUL, a Global Leader, knows his purpose is to reconcile people to God. 2 Corinthians 5:17-21

PETER, another Global Leader, focuses on our walk with and our reunion with Christ. I Peter 1:3-16

Action Steps

Ask yourself why you are in leadership and if you are eager to continue in that role. Do you like it? Why?

Be willing to ask others about your leadership skills and what abilities you need to work on. Ask for the negative as well as the positive comments.

Communicate what your purpose is, as Esther did, as you serve as a Global Leader. Tell others what you want to happen and see if they support where you are going.

Discipline yourself to be a learner. Study, read, pray, ask questions, watch other leaders, figure out what you have to do to be a good Global Leader. Never assume that you have arrived and are good enough!

Evaluate your purpose, your performance, your goals, your leadership, your motives on a regular basis. It would be great if you had a group of friends to help you do this.

Finish well! That has to be your overall purpose. That's what Esther wanted. Paul too! Read how Paul evaluated his Global Leadership in 2 Timothy 4:6-8.

A Leader Must Be QUICK

The concept of being "quick" might go against much of what you've learned about leadership and how you operate as an effective leader.

We're not talking about being "hasty," which means "hurried."

We're talking about your ability to respond to needs, opportunities and crisis quickly. This doesn't mean you rush through things and do it half-way.

We're talking about being ready to respond in a timely manner, and ready to make good, solid decisions, quickly.

This may be an issue of stewardship of our time or with our management style.

A Leader must be able to act quickly. There are things that come at you and sometimes the leader must be ready to make a quick and important decision or the opportunity goes by.

This is a tough one because we're all taught to be thoughtful, purposeful and intentional. All of these things are true.

However, there are also times that we are called to quick leadership and we have to be ready to respond, and confident enough in our leadership to not doubt ourselves.

How "quick" are you?

A Lesson From The Word

When I think about Jesus, I'm often amazed by how he responded to people. He was always looking for an opportunity to teach others, but sometimes his immediate response and quick action astounded those who were there.

In Luke 20:25 …Jesus responds to the scribes' question about paying taxes. Jesus asks for a coin and replies, "Then render to Caesar the things that are Caesar's, and to God the things that are God's." The people marveled at his answer.

Think of Jesus' quick responses to those who doubted him as he healed the paralytic in Mark 2 or how he defended Mary in Mark 14 for washing his feet with expensive perfume. Jesus always looked for opportunities to teach, to challenge, and to prove who he was.

Out of these and many more lessons, I think the Word is telling us to be ready. Be ready to respond when the opportunity is before us. Be ready to teach when people are listening.

2 Timothy 4:2 (NIV) says, "Preach the Word; be prepared in season and out of season; correct, rebuke and encourage—with great patience and careful instruction."

How Being Quick Will Help A Global Leader

Wouldn't it be nice if we had all the time in the world? Time to think, to process, to plan, to respond.

Time is something that we will always be lacking and as Global Leaders, the demands of everyday life crowd out our ability to take all the time we'd like to take to make decisions.

Making a quick decision doesn't mean that you aren't processing well. It simply means that you have prepared yourself and those around you to respond quickly to opportunities and challenges, and you're able to move when you're called upon.

I can't tell you how many times I've seen leaders miss wonderful opportunities, simply because they weren't ready to respond.

Our world is fast-paced. The needs are demanding.

Trust your leadership.

Be ready.

Be a leader.

Action Steps

1. Prepare.

In order to make quick decisions, you have to be ready. Surround yourself with people who you trust, people who are smarter than you, and people who can help you respond. Know your vision, know your call. Be confident in what you are doing and be ready to measure and evaluate things as they come to you.

2. Practice.

We're afraid to make quick decisions. Practice with small things and gain your confidence. Figure out what your limits and needs are and plan for them. Don't be afraid… try it!

3. Listen well.

The Bible tells us to be "quick to hear" the Word. Listen to what God is telling you. Listen to the voice of the Spirit in your life. Listen to those around you. Trust others' opinions, insights, and experience. You don't have to make these quick decisions on your own. Learn to listen to all that's going on around you. It will help you with every decision you are called on to make. Listen well.

A Leader Must Be
RELIABLE

The song, "Lean On Me," by Bill Withers, says, "Lean on me when you're not strong and I'll be your friend, I'll help you carry on for it won't be long 'til I'm gonna need somebody to lean on."

We all need people to help us carry on. We also need to be the kind of people who people can rely on.

If we make commitments that we don't keep, if we make promises only to break them, if our word is not solid, we will not have people to follow our lead.

Do your ministry partners trust you? Are you known as a leader whose word is true? Are you quick to promise and slow to deliver? Do you make promises to get out of a difficult situation only to break them later?

A Global Leader who can not be relied on is a leader no one will trust. A leader who can't be trusted will not be followed.

You must be reliable. You must do what you say you will do.

Being reliable is being dependable. People need that!

The smallest promise, the smallest commitment must have follow through by a leader. You cannot afford to be seen as someone whose word cannot be trusted. That means you must be careful what you agree to.

A Lesson From The Word

Philip was amazing!

Jesus had said that the Gospel would go to Samaria. (Acts 1:8) He needed someone to take it to a place most Jews didn't want to go. So, Philip went! Acts 8:4-5 (NLT) "But the believers who were scattered preached the Good News about Jesus wherever they went. Philip, for example, went to the city of Samaria and told the people there about the Messiah."

Then God needed someone to go down to the desert and tell one man from Ethiopia about Jesus. Philip went, Acts 8:26-27 (NLT) "As for Philip, an angel of the Lord said to him, 'Go south down the desert road that runs from Jerusalem to Gaza.' So he started out, and he met the treasurer of Ethiopia, a eunuch of great authority under the Kandake, the queen of Ethiopia. The eunuch had gone to Jerusalem to worship…"

Then, God needed someone in Azotus and then in the Roman colony of Caesarea, and there was Philip with his hand up. Acts 8:40 (NLT) "Meanwhile, Philip found himself farther north at the town of Azotus. He preached the Good News there and in every town along the way until he came to Caesarea."

Ever sung "Where you lead me I will follow?" Did you mean it?

A leader has to be willing to do anything to make it work.

How The Quality Of Reliability Will Affect The Global Leader

God needs Global Leaders He can trust. Leaders who have made the commitment to follow Him and then are reliable to do it anywhere He leads.

God needs Global Leaders who will do as He directs, even if it is hard or inconvenient or, even, impossible.

God needs Global Leaders who will do what He says when He says to do it. Wonder if Philip had decided to wait one day or one hour before he went to the desert as God directed? He would have missed the Ethiopian. He would have missed God's assignment and then wondered why God could not count on him. But, the Bible says "he ran" to obey God.

A Global Leader has to be consistent in follow Christ, he has to be consistent in doing what he says he will do, he has to stay on course and not get swayed from his purpose. People have to know where his commitments are, what his purpose is and who he is committed to.

A Global Leader must be reliable as a witness to the One he serves. If his word is not believed, then his message will not be accepted. If he doesn't keep his promises, people may assume that God doesn't keep His either. If he doesn't care for the needs of others, it may be said that neither does his God.

A Global Leader has to be who he says he is!!

Action Steps

First, check your commitments. What are you committed to? What promises have you made? Start with those close to you, your family. Ask them and make a list! Then move to those you work with. Those who help you do what you do. Those you are trying to reach. Go back through your history and list out the commitments.

Second, what are you going to do about them? Develop a plan to complete your commitments. Change your life style or schedule to be what you have promised to be. Make a list of what you need to do and start developing your plan to get it done.

Third, if some promises can't be kept today, work out a plan with the individual as to when you will keep it. Let them know that you remember the promise. Do not ignore any promise because it is hard. Work it out. You made the promise, now keep it!

Finally, be careful what promises you make because if you want to be seen as a Global Leader, you will want people to remember them and expect you to keep them. If you are not reliable you can damage all the work that God is trying to do through you. You can actually make Him look bad!

A Leader Must Be
SENSITIVE

Have you been told that showing your feelings and emotions is a sign of weakness? Do you believe that?

When you watch a movie that is either sad or moving, are you embarrassed by the small tear that forms in your eyes?

When did true emotion become such a negative thing?

Leaders must not only be aware of what's going on around them, but also must be able to feel what's going on around them.

Our culture and society has sensationalized everything to the extent that we aren't moved by much, unless it personally affects us.

What's wrong with feeling people's pain?

What's wrong with sharing emotion with those who are in the depths of despair?

Open your eyes! There's a lost and dying world all around you, and these people are desperate for hope, for truth and for life. Doesn't that bother you?

I'm not talking about your ability to cry in public. I'm talking about your ability to genuinely feel people's pain and sorrow as well as their joy and happiness.

What's your heart telling you?

A Lesson From The Word

In John 11, we read the story of Jesus' encounter with Mary and her sister Martha, centered around the death of their brother, Lazarus.

Jesus arrives on the scene after Lazarus has died and he encounters people who are in deep sorrow and grief.

Mary meets him and says in verse 32, "Lord, if you had been here, my brother would not have died." (ESV)

Jesus is moved by her weeping and sorrow, as well as the others' that are there, and the Bible tells us in verse 33 that "he was deeply moved in his spirit and greatly troubled."

Then, in verse 35, the powerful words, "Jesus wept." (ESV)

Jesus knows the end of the story. He knows of the coming resurrection and the joy that will come with new life.

Yet, at that moment, he faces deep sorrow with his friends at the reality of suffering and death.

Jesus, God as a man, feels their pain. He shares their pain. He comforts them.

Then, He does what only God can do: he turns their sorrow into dancing as Lazarus is brought back to life, from the dead.

What a day!

How Being Sensitive Will Help A Global Leader

People all over the world are in crisis and many of them simply need someone who will listen, someone who really cares, and someone who won't judge them. That's it.

Global Leaders have opportunities everyday to practice sensitivity. Look for it!

Here are some good questions to ask as you learn to be more sensitive:

1. What keeps you from responding to people who are in need?
2. What happens inside of you when you are "moved" by something? What is your first reaction?
3. What were you taught as a child when it comes to sharing emotionally? What's true and what's not true?
4. What drives you nuts about people's expression of sensitivity? What don't you like?

5. Think of someone you respect and think about how they model sensitivity. What do they do? Is it good and helpful?

Answer these questions and learn a little more about yourself and your ability to be sensitive as a leader.

Action Steps

1. Look around you.

Open your eyes to all that's around you. Sometimes we pass people in crisis every day, yet we're so busy and moving so quickly that we don't really see them and their need. Realize that there are people all around you who are hurting.

2. Ask yourself "what hurts the heart of God?"

Simply asking this question causes us to imagine what Christ would do? How would He respond? How would He show compassion? How would He show that He cares? If He does it, why don't you?

3. Practice sensitivity.

Take the initiative to show you care to people who are in crisis, or to people who are on top of the world. Figure out what being sensitive means for you. It might mean simply being available, it might mean asking the right questions, it might mean praying for that person. There are many ways to respond, but you need to figure out what that means for you, then do it.

A Leader Must Be
TEACHABLE

The definition of being teachable is: suitability for use in teaching, or ability to learn by instruction.

I would add: capable of being taught, apt and willing to learn, and favorable to teaching.

A Global Leader has to be a learner.

If a Global Leader thinks he has learned it all and has nothing else to learn, he is a fool and should not be in leadership.

We are living in a time when "change" is the descriptive word. In every area of our lives, things are changing. We have to keep learning just to keep up.

Global Leaders will often face situations they have never faced before. They will need help. They will need to ask for help. In those moments, they will learn how to deal with that situation the next time it comes. Then, and only then, will they be able to teach others. First, we learn and then we teach.

We teach by our words. We teach by our actions. We teach by our reactions. We teach by our attitudes. All these are seen and observed by our families, friends, co-workers, and enemies.

We teach others by everything we do. So, let's learn as much as we can so we can be the best teachers.

A Lesson From The Word

Joshua learned from Moses. Solomon learned from David. Gehazi learned from Elisha even as Elisha learned from Elijah.

Think of walking with Jesus along a road and listening to Him speak about what He saw and what He thought. The disciples were all learners and passed on what they learned. Now we have it from them.

Timothy learned from Paul. Read the letters Paul wrote to this young preacher/church leader. In those letters you will see the tasks necessary to be a Global Leader. (2 Timothy 4:1-2)

I solemnly urge you in the presence of God and Christ Jesus, who will someday judge the living and the dead when he appears to set up his Kingdom: Preach the word of God. Be prepared, whether the time is favorable or not. Patiently correct, rebuke, and encourage your people with good teaching. (2 Timothy 4:5)

But you should keep a clear mind in every situation. Don't be afraid of suffering for the Lord. Work at telling others the Good News, and fully carry out the ministry God has given you.

Where did Paul learn these things? He learned from his teacher, Barnabas, who befriended him right after he was saved (Acts 9:27). Barnabas spent a lot of time with Paul in those early days (Acts 11:25-26). He was with him in Jerusalem and again in Antioch. Barnabas and Paul even took that first missionary journey (2-3 years) together.

How The Quality Of Learning Will Affect The Global Leader

Just look at the examples of leaders in the Bible: Abraham, Joseph, Moses, Joshua, the good Kings, the judges, the prophets, so many others, all of them were learners. Most learned by watching the guy who went before them. Why do we think it is any different today?

Sometimes you want to be just like so and so, or you try not to do it the way they did it because it didn't work. Either way, a Global Leader learns by observing.

We learn how to communicate by listening and watching those who communicate.

We learn to plan by watching and learning from the good planners.

We learn to raise money by watching, asking and listening to the fund raisers.

A Global Leader does not have the luxury to say, "I can't." A Global Leader has to learn to do his best for the Kingdom. He may be the only one to do it, so he finds those who "can" and he learns from them.

The important thing for a Global Leader: He must admit what he doesn't know before he can learn. He has to do away with pride and be a learner.

Action Steps

Let's take the comments to Timothy as our outline:

Be prepared to learn. Be open to learn. Be anxious to learn. Set aside time to learn. Clear your schedule. Go to school!

Be ready because sometimes you will be learning by observing. You didn't even know there was going to be a lesson. You went to school on someone else's experience. Be a good observer. Keep quiet. Just learn.

Be patient. It won't all happen as fast as you want it to. You will still make mistakes and you will still need to admit, "I don't know!" But, as time goes by, you will better understand the right and wrong of a situation, of a decision, of an action. Encourage your family, and your staff, and those you are trying to reach as they see your growth and development. Encourage them as you teach them.

Be better than you are now! The more you learn:

- The better you will respond in different situations.
- The better you will think things through.
- The less uncertainly and insecurity you will experience.
- The better you will do at communicating what God wants you to communicate.

A Leader Must Be
USEFUL

We all want to be used by God. We want our lives to count for something, and we want to be used by God to impact His Kingdom and all of Eternity.

Sometimes in our quest to be used, we focus so much on what we can "do" that we forget to focus on who we need to "be."

Do you get caught up in that? Do you forget to stop to focus on your personal relationship with Christ and the disciplines in your life that help move you towards holiness?

This is a painful lesson to learn when you have to experience the pain of sin, brokenness, and failure because you didn't guard your lives from the attack of the enemy on a daily basis.

Jim Burns once said, "Unattended fires burn." He's talking about the need to take care of ourselves before we find ourselves burned out, taken out of the game, and un-useful to the master.

Today, take some time to reflect on where you're at in the personal management of your life. This includes soul care, your relationship with Christ, your relationship with those God has entrusted you with, and the integrity of your life.

How are you doing? Do you see any unattended fires?

A Lesson From The Word

II Timothy 2:20-26 (NASB)

Now in a great house there are not only vessels of gold and silver but also of wood and clay, some for honorable use, some for dishonorable. Therefore, if anyone cleanses himself from what is dishonorable, he will be a vessel for honorable use, set apart as holy, useful to the master of the house, ready for every good work.

So flee youthful passions and pursue righteousness, faith, love, and peace, along with those who call on the Lord from a pure heart. Have nothing to do with foolish, ignorant controversies; you know that they breed quarrels. And the Lord's servant must not be quarrelsome but kind to everyone, able to teach, patiently enduring evil, correcting his opponents with gentleness. God may perhaps grant them repentance leading to a knowledge of the truth, and they may come to their senses and escape from the snare of the devil, after being captured by him to do his will.

Do you want to be "useful to the master?"

Do you want to be "ready for every good work?"

Get your life in order!

How Being Useful Will Help A Global Leader

Think for a moment…

Think of three people you know personally who have "crashed and burned," people that were doing great things for the Lord, then something fell apart inside of them and they were unable to continue on in His service.

Think of three people you know personally who have been faithful to the task, who are grounded solidly in the Word, and are being used not only for what they can DO but for who they ARE. Can you think of them?

What differences do you see in the lives of these two groups of people?

What can you learn from the experiences of these people? Good and bad.

What are you doing today to keep yourself "USEFUL TO THE MASTER?"

We need more Global Leaders who are useful. We need leaders who are still in the game, who are taking care of themselves, and leaders who are pursuing holiness first, before addressing the needs and opportunities at hand.

Action Steps

1. Do you want to be used?

The first and most obvious question is simple. Do you really want to be used by God? Answer that question honestly. Sometimes we are really comfortable with the sin in our lives and we don't really want to change. We're content doing "good" things, but we aren't willing to work on who He wants us to "be." Answer this question before you move on.

2. Are you willing to work at it?

This takes work. It doesn't happen easily. It's not something you can focus on when you don't have anything else to do. Are you willing to really work on this? Are you willing to put the discipline in your life that will protect you and make you worthy of being used?

3. Do you have help?

Often, this is something that you can't do alone. You need others to walk with you. Do you have a group of people that you can be honest with? Is there someone who knows your deepest struggles and secrets? Is there someone who will walk with you and offer you accountability and support? Is there someone who will pray for you regularly and encourage you? You can't do this alone. Do you have the help to make it?

A Leader Must Have
VISION

Vision is when you can look at a problem and somehow work through the options to determine the solution.

Vision is the power of imagination, the ability to create ideas, situations, and/or solutions in your mind.

Vision is unusual discernment or foresight which must be credited to God. It's the ability to hear God, to see it from His point of view.

A Global Leader who is stuck in the past and living with the ideas and solutions of the past will watch his ministry become redundant and perhaps die.

A Global Leader who is living only in the present, perhaps fighting to stay afloat financially, not doing anything new or different will watch his ministry slowly grow stagnate.

A Global Leader who is looking around at problems that need to be solved and asks the question, "What can I do?" is a leader of an organization that will change and grow and become increasingly more effective.

Vision is what keeps us from being locked to our past history, or content with our current successes. Vision causes us to look ahead and to look around and to see the challenges and changes coming so we have time to react to them successfully.

A Lesson From The Word

The Bible has a lot to say about Vision:

The wisest man who lived tells us that where there is no vision, the people perish. (Proverbs 29:18)

Joseph was a great visionary. His brothers would say when they saw him coming: "Here comes that dreamer" (Genesis 37:19)

Elihu to Job, "Indeed God speaks once, or twice, yet no one notices it! In a dream, in a vision of the night, when sound sleep falls on men while they slumber in their beds, then He opens the ears of men, and seals their instruction, that He turn man aside from His conduct and keep man from his pride." (Job 33:14-17)

Joel tells us that "your old men WILL dream dreams, your young men WILL see visions." (Joel 2:28)

See yourself as a Child of God. (John 1:12)

See yourself representing Jesus and doing things just as He would do them. (II Corinthians 5:20)

See yourself as one "sent from God" to where you are today. (John 1:6)

See yourself committed to the Great Commission that He gave to each of us (Acts 1:8; Matthew 28:16-20; Luke 24:47; Mark 16:15; John 20:21-23)

How Vision Will Affect A Global Leader

A Global Leader must do more than run a ministry. He must do more than manage people. He must do more than balance a budget. A Global Leader has to have the ability to see the needs around him and adjust his ministry to respond to those needs.

To see the needs around him he needs to know what other ministries are doing. He has to know what the purpose of his ministry is. He needs to know what the commitments of his people are. He needs to know what fits and doesn't fit.

If the Global Leader sees a need that is not being resolved, one that he feels his ministry could speak to, then he must ask himself three simple questions:
1. What do these people need?
2. What can we do to respond to that need?
3. Where do we start?

He does not respond to the need to gain attention. He does not respond because it will bring in money. He only responds because God has told him to. This is a Global Leader with vision.

This kind of vision will cause his ministry to grow and always be relevant. This will allow his people to respond to real, current needs.

He will also be a Global Leader who God can trust with new vision.

Action Steps

Visualize what you think needs to be done. Ask the question, "What can I do?" instead of saying "Somebody ought to do something!"

Investigate what others are doing. You don't need to reinvent the wheel. If someone else is doing what you feel needs to be done, perhaps you can help them.

Schedule action steps…build a plan…talk about what God told you to do. Bring your staff together with you.

Initate think time and conversation. Accept other ideas. Let others become a part of solving this issue.

Own it! Don't pass it off! It is your vision! There is a reason God gave you the idea or vision. Like others in the Bible, He knows what you can do. Maybe you were put in the position you have for just this moment.

Never say "I can't"…you can through Christ! God will help you find your way through the obstacles and problems.—The better you will be at doing what God wants you to do! You can never know too much about serving God!

A Leader Must Be
WILLING

Sometimes as leaders, we like to have our job descriptions defined neatly and cleanly, clearly defining what it is we have to do in order to do our jobs.

The problem is that life is not like that.

There are times when we are called to step outside of our expected roles and do what it takes to get the job done.

We're not talking about distractions, about new opportunities, or about non-important things. We're talking about tasks and jobs that help to fulfill your vision and your goals.

There will be times that we don't have the manpower to get all that we need to get done, done. Matthew 9:37 tells us, "The harvest is plentiful, but the laborers are few." (ESV).

Are you willing to do what it takes to get the job done?

Are you willing to go above and beyond others' expectations in order to reach the goal?

Leaders must be willing to respond and to do what needs to be accomplished.

A Lesson From The Word

I Samuel 17: David and Goliath

There are so many lessons to learn from the story of David and Goliath. We can talk about the fear the Israelites had of Goliath. We can talk about God's faithfulness in granting David victory. We can talk about the "tools" David used to kill Goliath. All great stories.

One verse I want to focus on out of this story…

I Samuel 17:32 (ASV)

"And David said to Saul, "Let no man's heart fail because of him. Your servant will go and fight with this Philistine." Imagine the chaos of the scene:

- The armies had been facing off for over 40 days.
- Goliath taunted the Israelites, and they were all living in fear of what would happen when someone challenged Goliath.
- Then this child shows up, David, and without fear, he offers to go before this giant.

Where would you have been in this story?

Would you have joined the army of Israel in fear for your life?

Would you have been willing to do what needed to be done?

David was willing.

God granted him victory because of his willingness.

How Being Willing Will Help A Global Leader

There's a difference between "wanting" something and being "willing" to do whatever it takes.

Many of us "want" things to happen, "want" things to change, "want" things to grow.

Very few of us are "willing" to do whatever it takes to accomplish it.

Global Leaders often live and work in situations that require us to go above and beyond what we have signed up for. There will always be a shortage of people, a lack of resources, and time pressure. As leaders, we need to determine how we will respond. We have some choices:

- We can say, "Somebody needs to do something about that!"
- We can say, "I can't!"
- We can say, "It's not my job!"

Or if it's something that is important, something that moves us towards our goals and vision, and something that impacts lives, we can say, "I'm WILLING!"

Are you willing?

Action Steps

1. Do you wait for others to respond first?

When you're willing, you respond first. Don't wait for others. If there's something to do that needs to be done, do it. Don't evaluate it, don't assume someone else will do it. You do it.

2. Do you blame others for not responding?

We can spend a lot of time and energy blaming others and complaining that others aren't doing their share. Don't fall into this trap. Lead by example, even when the task is not your job. Others will follow. Servant Leadership is the ability to do whatever it takes for the good of the organization and the team. Sometimes it means you do the worst jobs. Don't let pride keep you from being a leader.

3. Are you afraid?

Fear has a way of paralyzing us. It keeps us from doing things that we know we should not be doing. Learn to identify fear in your life, and don't let it keep you from moving. When fear comes, talk it through. Identify where it's coming from, if it's rational and what you should do about it. Our first response when fear comes is to simply say "NO." Before you say no, think it through. Don't let fear win!

A Leader Must Be
XEROGRAPHIC

This word is a noun. It describes an electrostatic printing process for copying text or graphics whereby areas on a sheet of paper corresponding to the image areas of the original are sensitized with a charge of static electricity so that, when powdered with a toner carrying an opposite charge, only the charged areas retain the toner, which is then fused to the paper to make it permanent.

So here you are and there Jesus is and you want to be like Him. Impossible! But then the "charger," the Holy Spirit, gets involved. He hears our response as we become "sensitized" by the Spirit of God who puts in us the desire to be like Jesus. The "static electricity" of our lives is the Holy Spirit cleansing our lives with the "toner," His voice, in our hearts. He is the one who will take our sinful life and "fuse" it to Jesus. That's when we reflect Christ!

We are like a clean piece of paper put through a machine, copying the exact image of another sheet of paper (Jesus) that is put in the machine with us.

A Global Leader just can't do it all by himself. He has to look for examples, models of leadership that he can copy to do a better job at what God has called him to do.

The Global Leader who does not feel the need to be a better leader will fail in his leadership.

A Lesson From The Word

Paul tells the church in Corinth that they "should imitate me, just as I imitate Christ." I Corinthians 11:1 (NLT)

He tells the church in Thessalonica that they should do the same. "For you know that you ought to imitate us or follow our example." II Thessalonians 3:7 (NLT)

Then he tells the church in Ephesus how: "Imitate God, therefore, in everything you do, because you are his dear children. Live a life filled with love, following the example of Christ. He loved us and offered himself as a sacrifice for us, a pleasing aroma to God. Let there be no sexual immorality, impurity, or greed among you. Such sins have no place among God's people. Obscene stories, foolish talk, and coarse jokes—these are not for you. Instead, let there be thankfulness to God. You can be sure that no immoral, impure, or greedy person will inherit the Kingdom of Christ and of God. For a greedy person is an idolater, worshiping the things of this world." Ephesians 5:1-5 (NLT)

Could we ever tell the people we work with that they should imitate us? They should copy the way we react, the way we respond, the way we work, the way we speak?

The secret, as Paul said, was to "imitate me as I imitate God."

First, he wanted to be like Jesus. Then, he wanted us to be like Jesus as well. Not a bad goal!

How The Quality Of Xerographic Will Affect A Global Leader

The world around us is in a constant stage of change!

The Global Leader who does not feel the need to grow and change will grow redundant and he will fail in his leadership.

We must always watch other leaders and study the qualities that make them successful. I believe that copying the leadership qualities of another leader is the highest form of compliment.

To do this, we must know and admit that there are some things we do not do well, areas in which we are not strong leaders. We must be willing to work on those areas to improve our leadership skills.

To do that we must be willing to change.

Change will only happen when we desire to be better. Not for more glory or praise, but to be more effective in our calling. God wants to help us be better. He will help us see the qualities, in others, and in Christ that will make us better leaders.

"The one who calls you is faithful and He will do it!" II Thessalonians 5:24

Action Steps

CHRIST is the ultimate leader. With a handful of men He changed history and the course of life. There is no better leader to copy, so don't hesitate to ask, "What would Jesus do?" or "Would Jesus do it this way?"

Obey the voice of the Holy Spirit. He will speak to you in your mind, through the Bible or with the voice of another person. He is the "charger" in your life and He will be the one who helps you be a better leader.

Put value on other leaders. They were put there by God just as you were put where you are. Don't envy their position or organization. Don't compete with them. Don't be negative toward them. They are all there by design, for you to copy or perhaps as an example of the kind of leader you are not to be.

Yield to the standard set by God in His Word. It tells us to: (1) Live a life filled with love, following the example of Christ. (2) Let there be no sexual immorality, impurity, or greed among you. (3)Instead, let there be thankfulness to God.

God has given you a great opportunity to lead others. Ask God to change you into the best leader you can be.

A Leader Must
YIELD

The definition we're going to use with the word yield is: "To make way; to give the right of way; to allow."

Sometimes, yielding is difficult for us as leaders. We like to be in charge, we like to be the center of attention, we like to be the focus.

A real leader must be willing to step up when they have to, but has to be willing and able to allow others to lead as well.

So many times we as leaders believe that it's all about us. We lead as if the world would fall apart if we weren't there to make that decision or to motivate people. Sometimes we forget that there are other leaders around us, and we need to make space for them to learn to lead, and to lead.

Yielding is difficult.

Our ego comes into play when others get the attention we often want and deserve.

Our pride gets in the way as we think about how we could have done something better than the other leader.

Are you willing to share leadership?

Are you willing to make space for others to express the gifts they've been given?

A Lesson From The Word

In John 3 we read an amazing exchange between John the Baptist and his disciples concerning Jesus. John the Baptist is explaining who Christ is and why He is to be "above all." Look at some of the words he uses:

Vs. 28 I am not the Christ, but I have been sent before him.

Vs. 30 He must increase, but I must decrease.

Vs. 31 He who comes from above is above all.

Vs. 31 He who comes from heaven is above all.

John has clearly defined his role as preparing the way for the Lord, and when the time comes, he graciously steps down, exalting Jesus to all he comes in contact with, and stepping off of the center stage.

John's disciples challenge this, yet John knows his place, knows his role, and knows who Jesus really is.

He yields. He gets out of the way.

How Yielding Will Help A Global Leader

Jim Burns teaches one aspect of "yielding" and he calls it DELEGATION. Often, we want to simply hand leadership off without going through a process of teaching and modeling leadership. Global Leaders have to learn to delegate.

Here are Jim's 4 phases:

1. I Do It, You Watch
The first step is to invite people in, close to you, to watch you lead.

2. I Do It, You Do It
Allow others to lead with you, sharing the decisions, sharing the opportunities.

3. You Do It, I Help You
Allow others to actually "take" the leadership, and you stick with them to support them and to help them if they need it.

4. You Do It, I Do Something Else
As they learn to lead and assume the leadership, you are able to focus on other things.

This model is a model of growth, of empowerment and of yielding your leadership to others in a healthy way. Make space for others. Allow them to lead.

Action Steps

1. Know your role.

An important place to start is simply in knowing your role, knowing your strengths, and knowing how you lead. Knowing these things will help you as you work with other leaders.

2. Identify other leaders.

When we talk about making space for others to lead, we're not talking about allowing anyone to do anything. You must invest your time and energy in identifying the "right" leaders...people who have gifts, desire and who are willing to put the work into it. When you find these people, then you begin to give them space to lead and you help them grow in their leadership.

3. Make space.

When we "yield," we're not talking about just giving people the jobs that we don't want. Yielding is allowing people to work in their strengths, even when that competes with your strengths as the leader. Be confident in who you are, so confident that you're not threatened when you make space for someone else to lead and they actually do a better job than you would have done. Celebrate their success. Cheer them on. Affirm them. That's what leaders do!

A Leader Must Be
ZEALOUS

A boring, static leader is a leader no one wants to follow unless they realize they only have one life and the time is short while the needs are many.

People who want to make a difference want a leader with zeal for what God has called him to. They want a leader who is excited about his job, his responsibility, because he sees God in his calling and in his work.

God says it is His zeal that accomplishes what He does. He wants to put His zeal in every leader He calls. A spiritual fervor for what he is doing, a leader who is never lacking in that zeal, always anxious to serve the Lord.

Without that zeal of the Lord, the leadership job could become just another job. We would see more problems than blessings. We would worry, we may even be "weary in well doing." Our reward system would be polluted.

There has to be excitement in the leader's task to "contend earnestly for the faith" in whatever his assignment might be. In fact, the zeal of the Lord will keep him from getting distracted by the problems and missing the assignment all together.

God needs leaders who lead with His zeal, a leader with an eagerness and ardent interest in doing what God wants!

A Lesson From The Word

Isaiah tells us several times that "The ZEAL of the Lord Almighty will accomplish this…" (Isaiah 37:32; 9:7)

What God does, in us and around us, He does with zeal!

Jeru, the King of Israel, said, "Come with me and see my zeal for the Lord" (2Kings 10:16) Would we ever say something like that? Do we have zeal or excitement for the Lord that people can see?

Paul tells us to "Never be lacking in zeal, but keep your spiritual fervor, serving the Lord" (Romans 12:11)

God told Moses that he was pleased with his nephew, Phinehas, because "he was as zealous as I am for the honor of his God" (Numbers 25:11-13)

Perhaps the best example was the brother of Jesus, who wrote: "Dear friends, I had been eagerly planning to write to you about the salvation we all share. But now I find that I must write about something else, urging you to defend (Contend earnestly) the faith that God has entrusted once for all time to his holy people." (Jude 1:3)

Having zeal, spiritual fervor, for the faith will always involve contending for the faith. It also will be powered by God's zeal if anything is to get done. Oh, that all would see our zeal for the Lord!

How The Quality Of Zeal Will Affect A Global Leader

God works with the leader. We see that throughout history in the Bible.

First, there were the patriarchs, Abraham, Issac and Jacob. Through them He spoke to the people.

Second, there were the Judges, like Gideon, Deborah, Samson and Samuel, among others.

Third, there were the Kings, some good and some bad.

Along with the Kings, there were prophets, speaking the zeal of the Lord to the people.

The names that we know, we know because of their zeal for the Lord! Or we know their names because of their disobedience of the Lord's commands. It is always one or the other. What will you be known for?

Paul talks about apostles, evangelists, pastors, and teachers, all leaders in the church. (Ephesians 4:11)

If you, as a Global Leader of a ministry, want to make a difference in the world while you are here, you will only do it as you let the zeal of the Lord work through you. There is zeal in doing things His way as you serve Him! Get excited about your calling to lead!

Action Steps

To get the zeal of the Lord you need to ask for it!

To get the zeal of the Lord in your leadership you need to submit your leadership to Him. You will need to do things His way. You will need to do the things He would do. You will need to focus on the needs that He would focus on. You need to give Him the praise!

Jude tell us we need to do 6 things to be "Contenders"

1. (:17) Remember what God has said to us...get in His Word and let His Word in us!

2. (:20) Build yourselves up in the faith...Don't blame others for our failures. Set a spiritual goal we know we need to grow!

3. (:20) Pray in the Holy Spirit...Set a time and a place to pray!

4. (:21) Keep yourself in God's love...Clean up a negative attitude, a jealousy or a bitterness!

5. (:22) Be merciful...Restore a broken relationship. You make the first move!

6. (:23) Hating even the clothing stained…Get rid of one thing you know offends God.

It takes zeal, the zeal of the Lord, to be a contender. If you are not a contender, why are you in leadership? Step aside.

Leadon Esource

The Leadon Esource pages have been created to help leaders around the world to grow in their leadership and to have access to practical tools that will help in leading their organizations.

The team of people that contribute to these pages have a wide variety of leadership, cross-cultural, and organizational experience. It's our desire to provide ongoing resources to leaders who desperately need help and support.

www.leadonesource.org

www.facebook.com/leadonesource

@leadonesource

About the Authors

Russ Cline

Russ' passion is providing leaders around the world with the support, encouragement and partnership they desperately need. His background in organizational development, leadership training and cross-cultural partnerships enable him to encourage, train and coach leaders around the world. Beyond this, Russ is Ron's son. www.extremeresponse.org

Ron Cline

A man gifted in communicating the gospel of Jesus Christ, Dr. Ronald A. Cline challenges and edifies the body of Christ. His background as a pastor, educator, counselor, missionary and author gives him credibility and rapport with the many groups and individuals he and his wife, Barbara, minister to around the world each year. www.hcjb.org